DEDICATION

To Janelle and Linda who have given me grace and patience to 'make this thing work'.

Hidden Skills: Uncovering What Your Business Really Needs

Solo Entrepreneurs Ready to Scale

Roxanne Massey

Copyright © 2024 Roxanne Massey

All rights reserved.

www.honesthr.co.uk

CONTENTS

1	Introduction	1
2	The Myths: What you've been told	Pg 2
3	Conducting a Skill Gap Analysis	Pg 13
4	Creating Compelling Job Descriptions	Pg 27
5	Mastering the Interview Process	Pg #
6	Implementing Effective Onboarding and Integration	Pg 34
7	Maintenance	Pg 47
8	FAQs	Pg 49
9	Outro	Pg 56

1 Introduction

Imagine hitting a wall in your entrepreneurial journey. You know you have the passion, drive, and vision, but something isn't clicking. It's not going how you planned or as swiftly as you expected.

That was me.

After countless sleepless nights trying to figure out why my business wasn't scaling, I had my eureka moment.

The missing piece?

A deep understanding of the skills my business needed but didn't have.

Honestly, I felt a little foolish. I'm trained in business strategy and HR, so why wasn't I implementing what I knew into my business? Sigh. After all, I do this in other companies, so why not my own?

This realisation led me on a quest to identify these skills and master the art of integrating them into my business.

This journey wasn't easy; self-reflection can be challenging but transformative.

Now, I want to share this blueprint with you.

This is the culmination of my experiences and education, designed to fast-track your success and help you achieve the work-life balance you, yes you, deserve.

You haven't just bought a product; you're stepping onto a path I've paved with trials, errors, and successes. Let me guide you through making your business everything you've dreamed it could be.

2 THE MYTHS: WHAT YOU'VE BEEN TOLD

Myth 1: Entrepreneurs often turn into overnight successes.

Reality: it's rarely overnight; it just looks like it is, and I mean rare. Entrepreneurs have worked hard in the background (like you and I) forever.

The myth of the lone wolf conquering the business world alone is prevalent and romanticised.

But here's the unglamorous truth: scaling a business is a team sport. It's not about working harder but working smarter with the right people by your side.

When rolling solo, you are every person on the team: operations, sales, marketing, finance, and IT. Doing every job can get you so far, as can automation, but there comes a time when No one is an expert in every area, and it's okay to have gaps in our skills.

In reality, what may look like someone suddenly taking their niche by storm is more likely the work and effort of countless long days, late nights and dedication—followed by the right break happening and the PR wheels going in full motion.

Myth 2: More experience equals better performance

Reality: Experience is important but only sometimes guarantees better performance. Have you heard the idea that you need to do something for 10,000 hours to become an expert? It may be true, but do you have that many hours for each area of your business?

When outsourcing some of your support work, you may want an expert. Or you may opt for someone you can train to be the best you need.

However, adaptability, cultural fit, and growth potential often play a more significant role in long-term success.

A focused process that assesses these qualities can lead to more effective hiring decisions than experience alone.

Myth 3: Skill gaps are primarily a hiring issue

Reality: Many believe that you can solve skill gaps solely through hiring.

When it's just you in the business, you can seek personal training to fill in some of your gaps. If you have enough demand, you can outsource some elements to specialists or hire a team member.

You can pool your talents to help fill gaps when you have a team.

A holistic approach to identifying and filling skill gaps ensures a balanced strategy utilising internal and external resources.

Myth 4: Hiring Quickly Is Always Better

Reality: When you've decided to get some support, it can instantly feel like you needed them to start yesterday. I know, I've been there. All those tasks that are now on your new hires' to-do list seem like too much for you to do; you just want them to start ASAP.

The pressure to fill positions rapidly can lead to rushed hiring decisions, potentially compromising quality.

Finding the right fit, even if it takes longer, saves resources in the long run by reducing turnover and improving team dynamics.

You may wait a while longer to find someone with the right cultural fit, passing on the person who has all the skills but may not suit the working environment. Equally, you may take on the person who has a great cultural fit and has the skills you are actively trying to fill but needs some others that you can upskill them on.

A streamlined yet thorough hiring process balances speed with quality.

Myth 5: A Good Curriculum Vitae (CV/ Resume) Guarantees a Good Hire

Reality: A resume provides a snapshot of a candidate's background but doesn't capture their work ethic, team dynamics, or problem-solving abilities.

If you decide to hire someone, whether outsourcing to a freelancer, agency, part-time or full-time in-house, you should do more than look at their CV to determine if they are the right person for you.

Incorporating practical assessments and behavioural interviews into the hiring process offers a more comprehensive view of a candidate's potential.

Myth 6: Onboarding Is Just Paperwork and Procedures

Reality: Onboarding is mistakenly seen as a checkbox exercise focused on logistics and paperwork. In reality, it starts before the person has even been hired.

When deciding on a position to fill, a list of things the person will need to have a successful start will accompany it.

First impressions do not start on day one; they start before the interview. How you present your business begins when the advert is first seen. It could be even earlier if you have a visible online or store-front presence.

We want to ensure that every interaction is an authentic presentation of the culture we are building, our vision, mission and values and to follow this into our onboarding process.

Effective onboarding is crucial for cultural integration and long-term retention. It involves personalised training, mentorship, and gradual immersion into the company culture.

A process that values these aspects can significantly improve employee engagement and productivity.

Myth 7: Interviews Are the Best Way to Assess Skills

Reality: Traditional interviews focus on verbal responses and can miss critical elements of a candidate's capabilities, especially for practical or technical skills.

It's important to remember that people have different capabilities, especially in a pressured environment like an interview. Some people may not excel in an interview but are perfect for a position. For this reason, we should have a varied approach to the interview process and be consistent with our strategy for all candidates.

Incorporating work samples, trials, or project-based assessments can provide a more accurate picture of a candidate's abilities and fit.

Myth 8: Soft Skills Aren't As Important As Hard Skills

Reality: There's a growing misconception that hard skills trump soft skills in technical roles. The reality is that soft skills often complement technical skills in many areas, including the professional work environment.

However, soft skills like communication, adaptability and patience often differentiate a good employee from a great one.

To expand on this:

Communication: Clear and effective communication allows for effective teamwork and reduced misunderstandings. Ideas are easily conveyed, and problem-solving is facilitated.

Adaptability: This will allow people to pivot with the changes often happening with smaller businesses; rapidly embracing change and uncertainties will allow for dynamic environments.

Patience: If you hire someone to work on the front line and deal with your customers, whether in person or online, you will want them to display customer service skills. In addition to technical skills, patience, empathy, and listening are vital soft skills.

Evaluating both hard and soft skills with equal rigour ensures a well-rounded team.

Myth 9: The Best Talent Is Always Actively Looking for Jobs

Reality: The assumption that top talent is actively job hunting overlooks passive candidates who might be open to new opportunities but aren't actively applying. Even if the top talent was actively looking, they are likely to see only some positions available, and they may be looking in a slightly different area, salary bracket, or other variables.

Engaging with and nurturing talent pools, including passive candidates, can uncover exceptional talents who weren't on your radar. They may not be looking to move right now, and you may not be looking to hire right now, but nurturing what we call your talent pool keeps communications close for when the time is right. Your talent pool is a quirky way to call a group of people who may be interested in working for you at some point.

Myth 10: Skill Development Is Solely the Employee's Responsibility

Reality: Companies sometimes believe that employees should take the initiative for their growth, and they should indeed lead their personal development. However, only they know what they want or don't want.

While self-motivation is important, employers are crucial in providing opportunities, resources, and support for continuous learning and development. We want to help guide our team to make the best decisions for them, see where that may fit into our business model, and support them accordingly. You may find that what someone wants does not exist within your business, but we can still help either way. Guidance can still be provided; they will likely learn elements that can be used within your company, too, even if it only appears to be soft skills. You don't have to commit to spending money; providing time is beneficial too.

Myth 11: More Training Is the Solution to Every Skill Gap

Reality: While training is vital, only some skill gaps can be bridged through courses or workshops.

Sometimes, restructuring teams, adding team members, enhancing collaboration, or leveraging technology can be more effective solutions.

Adding an increasing number of skills to a particular job may push it towards a different role with a higher salary, which either of you may not desire. More tasks will take away from other tasks currently being completed.

A strategic approach assesses the nature of the gap and the best way to address it, which may only sometimes mean more training.

3 Conducting a Skill Gap Analysis

Knowing your destination is as important as knowing your starting point in any journey. When you started your business, it may have been with a big vision in mind. Perhaps you wanted to solve a problem, something you knew you could do better than others. Even if you fell into your business unintentionally, you have made it this far.

As an entrepreneur, you will often find yourself doing more tasks than a typical 9-5 job, covering more areas and skills, and as much as we may not want to admit it, we have gaps in our knowledge. Our knowledge gaps must be filled to allow us to reach our destination. Before we can identify where the gaps are, we need to be able to define where we want to go clearly. This will allow us to set the stage for success, aligning our business capabilities with our overall strategic objectives.

To bridge the gap between our current abilities and future needs, we will define the skills essential for achieving our business goals. Completing this step will provide a targeted approach for developing the needed skills and ensure that every activity takes you closer to achieving your business ambitions.

This initial phase will involve a deep dive into your business plans, projecting your future needs and the roles that may be needed to meet those needs. We will look beyond the day-to-day tasks that you complete and strategically look at the bigger picture.

For a long time, I swayed away from my business goals, chasing income and clients, moving away from what I wanted to be doing. It is easy to get caught up in the day-to-day activities of your business, forgetting to look at whether these steps are bringing you closer to your goal and if they are still aligned with what you want to do or be. I worked in rather than on my business.

Let's explore how we can survive and thrive in business, lay down these foundational objectives and identify the critical skills that will propel your business forward.

Step 1: Define Business Objectives and Desired Skills

Let's begin by doing some strategic thinking and planning. We will momentarily step out of the day-to-day operations to examine your long-term business objectives and the skills needed. Looking ahead will help by setting the stage for where the business is and where it needs to be, envisioning your desired outcomes, and creating a plan to achieve them.

Shifting your focus from day-to-day operations to long-term strategic planning is crucial. This will allow you to understand how your business operates now and envision how it should operate in the future, with a plan for adapting.

Let's identify and articulate your clear business goals.

1. Stakeholders: Gather anyone you would classify as a key stakeholder in your business. As an entrepreneur, you may be alone; you may have a business partner or a supportive friend who can help you brainstorm. If you already have a team, bring along the heads of each business section, for example, your lead marketing or finance person. You may need to break this activity down into different sessions.

2. Vision: Clearly articulate where you see your business in the future. This is your vision; it should be inspirational and be your guiding star for setting goals.

Examples of visions:

To redefine fashion e-commerce by offering an exclusive selection of handcrafted, sustainable garments that empower artisans worldwide and inspire consumers to make conscious style choices.

To innovate everyday processes through software solutions that enhance productivity and creativity, starting with solo professionals and small businesses as the cornerstone of a digitally empowered future.

To lead small businesses toward a green future by providing

actionable, customised sustainability practices that save the planet and enhance business efficiency and community reputation.

3. Objectives: It is time to break down that vision into specific goals. We want to have short (1 year), medium (3 years) and long-term (5 years) goals.

   Each goal must be clear and aligned with the broader overall vision and will form your objectives; it must also be measurable. This means that you need to be able to measure whether you have achieved it or not. You can do this by having a figure to achieve, whether financial or percentage. By adding a key result to your objectives, you will have your OKR. Your OKRs are a method that you can use to keep track of how well you are sticking to your vision.

When reviewing the goals, decide what initial skills will be needed for each area based on your current knowledge. As you progress, you will identify new skills to develop, which is okay.

Short-term goals should focus on actionable and immediate objectives to achieve medium-term goals. You will need to determine what skills, such as marketing, sales, product development, or customer service skills, are necessary to achieve these goals.

Medium-term goals should act as milestones that progress you towards your long-term goals. More strategic skills, such as strategic leadership or operational management, are needed here.

Long-term goals should align with and lead you to your vision. For longer-term goals, you may need further advanced skills, such as advanced technological skills, innovation management, and complex problem-solving abilities.

Examples of goals:

Small-term goals

- Hit a revenue milestone, e.g. earning a certain amount within the year

- Increase customers by 40% through targeted marketing campaigns and social media outreach.
- Double the number of website visitors through SEO improvements and content marketing.
- Introduce a loyalty program to increase repeat customers by 30%
- Launch a new service or product that addresses a clear market need, backed by customer research and feedback.

Medium-term goals

- Launch a new product line that complements existing offers, targeting a new segment.
- Establish critical partnerships with key industry players to enhance brand recognition.
- Reduce operating costs by 25% through improvements in operations.
- Obtain relevant industry certifications to enhance credibility.

Long-term goals

- Expand sales to include customers in over 50 countries, focusing on growing markets.
- Develop a technology to set an industry standard, ensuring a competitive edge.
- Become a household brand name known for quality and reliability in the market.

4. Skills mapping: Now that you have your goals/objectives, it's time to do some skills mapping. This will involve understanding what skills are required to achieve each objective; more than one skill may be required. Each objective will require a unique set of skills. We are not looking for what skill is missing; we want to know the crucial skill required, whether it is missing or not. These skills may

be technical or soft skills such as leadership or communication.

Brainstorm thoroughly through the skills necessary for the objectives. If one of your objectives is to increase customers through website marketing, a crucial skill required would be content writing/marketing.

5. Evaluating skills: Next to each skill, starting with the short-term objectives, you should assess:

   The importance of the skill to achieve the objective: High/Medium/Low

   The urgency of the skill to accomplish the objective: High/Medium/Low

   Assess the current level of this skill (you or others in your team): Strong/Average/Weak.

Having completed these initial steps, you will have a strategic foundation for the following stages. Get ready to prioritise your skill development and maximise your business's growth.

Step 2: Assessing current skills

We know how we want our future to turn out, and we can see what initial skills we need to achieve our desired success.

Assessing our current skill set and requirements, we see that some tasks may be more challenging than others.

A good practice is to have an operations manual of your business so that as you grow, you can pass on the 'manual' to people to pick up and complete the tasks easily. This could be written in a document or recorded as a video.

To help you grow your business, you must understand what you do and how long it takes. An excellent way to do this is to list all your tasks, preferably grouping them by type of work, such as, financial or marketing tasks.

- Write down a specific step-by-step guide, missing nothing out, for every activity you do in your business.

- Next to your list, which may appear quite long if you do various tasks, you should highlight the primary skill required to complete the task (as we did before) and your confidence level in completing the task. You can use our dedicated resource or complete it using a method that suits you best.

If other people within your business are completing the tasks for you, you can also assess them based on their skill levels. You can do this through regular reviews, asking them in a sit-down meeting about their confidence levels, gathering feedback, and having staff complete self-evaluation surveys. If you take this approach, you must include them in the process so they do not feel threatened by any changes you make. As you grow bigger, there are specific company tools you can use that will help you analyse your team's strengths.

Having completed this assessment, we do not need to make any assumptions about what we should focus on with skills development. We can conduct an evidence-based analysis of the current and potential future.

Step 3: Identify Skills Gaps

With the foundational work completed, we now have two lists, one of the skills required for our future growth and the other of our current skills position, prioritised. We now approach a pivotal step of identifying the gaps between our current capabilities and the skills our business needs to succeed. Our critical thinking and problem-solving skills will come in handy here to help us pinpoint and prioritise specific developmental areas which are most urgently needed.

By mapping out and assessing skill discrepancies that could hinder business objectives and progression, we can compare our existing skills against those required for future success. We can understand the precise gaps and the impact on our strategic goals. This process is more than looking for deficiencies; it is about creating opportunities for growth and competitive advantage.

Gather the information you have collected about your current and future skill set. We want to see the skills needed to grow visually and where we currently are.

1. Layout. You could add an extra column to a document you have created to see any gaps, e.g. Copywriting skill required, current skill level = 2, level of skill needed = 5.
2. Another method is to create a chart in your chosen spreadsheet tool or a table on pen and paper. Choose whichever method is most comfortable for you.
3. Assess each gap based on its severity to your business's growth. This will help you prioritise which skill you address first. Consider factors like the skill's importance to the business's core operations, the consequences of keeping the gap as it currently is, and the difficulty of closing it. Closing the gap may require training; consider how long the training may take and how much time you have.
4. Categorise the gap. Next to each skill, put a category related to the relevant business function, e.g. sales, finance, management, Operations, and technology. While you may still need to get these departments, we are starting to think about how the business will expand.

Step 4: Prioritise Skills Gaps

You should now clearly understand the existing business skills and the gaps we face; the next step is prioritising these gaps. This step will be crucial because it will help us to determine which skills gaps are the most critical and should be addressed first, allowing us to drive the most significant impact on our business's success.

Here, we will take a systematic approach to evaluate the potential impact of each identified gap on our business operations. We are not here to simply acknowledge any deficiencies; we will strategically decide where to allocate our limited resources to maximise business performance by categorising and prioritising each skill gap based on its urgency and importance to the business objectives.

This step will take us from being aware of our gaps to creating actionable insights to direct our resources to areas of greatest need. It will provide a clear roadmap of priorities that will guide our training, hiring and development investments. This careful planning ensures that our actions are strategic and aligned with our overarching business goals, setting the stage for effective execution and measurable improvements.

1. Assess the impact of each gap that you have identified. We want to think about what impact there will be on the business if the absence of these skills remains. Consider the answers to these questions:
    a. How does this gap impact our ability to meet current and future business objectives?
    b. If we do not address these gaps in the short or long term, what will be the risk to the business?
2. Create a Priority Matrix. We can create a priority matrix to represent what to focus on visually. A priority matrix is a square divided into four, like a traditional window shape. Each corner holds a different level of priority.
    a. Bottom left—Low impact, low urgency—This quadrant has the lowest priorities. If we were to implement any skills gap in this section, it would have minimal impact and be the least urgent. Put any skill gap in here that you have marked as low in urgency and impact.

    b. Bottom right—Low impact, high urgency—In this quadrant, you need to place the skills gaps with the lowest impact on the business. If you were to implement them, they may provide quick fixes that would improve daily operations. These gaps are less critical, and maybe something like automating tasks is not a priority but will free up time and make life easier.
    c. Top left - High impact, low urgency - This quadrant contains important gaps. They may not require immediate action from you, but they are crucial for the long-term success of your business.
    d. Top right - High impact, high urgency - This quadrant is where you place the gaps that need immediate attention to avoid significant disruption to your business.

Over time, you may have fewer items in your high impact, high urgency section, which is excellent as it means that you are no longer fire-fighting things to do. This will allow you to prioritise gaps in the high-impact, low-urgency section. This will mean that you have a less stressful situation trying to rescue your business and will be able to work on strategic tasks that will improve your business's overall position instead.

3. Criteria. Now that you can see the skills gaps in your high impact, high urgency, top right quadrant, you can create criteria for how you would like to prioritise these skills gaps. Consider which of these or other things you would like to prioritise:
    a. Freeing up your time
    b. Return on investment
    c. Customer impact
    d. Legal or compliance requirements.

You may find that it is most important to free up your time, whether to focus on other tasks that bring money into your business or to reduce the time you spend working.

Perhaps your most significant gap, with the highest

priority, involved improving sales skills. Closing this gap through training or hiring someone may provide a great return on investment, which could be the first focus.

If you struggle to keep up with your customers, you may prioritise tasks with the highest customer impact.

Alternatively, you may need better compliance or legislation changes. This could be a priority to work on, which, while not increasing income, ensures that you remain compliant within your business.

You could prioritise other item groups, and that is acceptable—group your skills gaps by priority from the matrix and by criteria.

Give each criterion a score of importance. Focus first on the highest-criterion quadrant in the top right, high-impact, high-urgency quadrant, working your way down to the lowest-criterion quadrant. Then, do the same through the remaining quadrants.

You may write this out as a list in order, but remember that priorities could change as you work through them, and new gaps could emerge.

4. Create an action plan. For each item on your list, you need to decide whether to focus on
    a. Training
    b. Hiring or
    c. Outsourcing to close the gap.

If you have limited funds and cannot hire someone, personal training is the route until you can grow to a stage where you can hire or outsource. You may have some funds and potentially irregular income; this could be ideal for outsourcing tasks as project work. Here, someone could come into your business to complete a small bulk of functions for you, freeing up your time with less financial commitment. Give each task a timeline for completion; this may change your options. If training up on a gap takes two years, you may find outsourcing or hiring someone beneficial.

5. Transparency—If you have other people within your business, this would be a good time to share your analysis and decisions with them. Being transparent will help them understand your steps, the rationale behind prioritising them, and how they are being addressed.

Step 5: Develop strategies to close skill gaps

You have a great action plan almost ready to go, so it's time to translate our insights into concrete, actionable plans. Whether choosing personal training, strategic hiring, or innovative outsourcing, each approach will be tailored to address the gap and align with the overall business goals.

In the previous step, you identified the best approach to closing each gap. Now, we will examine each one slightly more closely.

Options - Confirm which option you will take to close the gap:

Training and Development - These skills can be developed internally; you can design a training program if you train others. You could source relevant training programs, either in person or online, for yourself or others. This could be a technical course, leadership training, or soft skills training.

Hiring new employees - If you have skills that are critically lacking or cannot be developed internally within a reasonable timeframe, hiring new employees may be your best option. It would help if you created a detailed job description that accurately reflects the required skills and experience to do this.

Outsourcing - This is an excellent option for project-specific skills or when funds are limited to hire staff. Consider outsourcing to freelancers or firms that specialise in the required area.

Timelines - You should establish a realistic timeline for each strategy. Setting clear milestones and deadlines will keep you on target for starting, completing key milestones and completing the step (closing the gap). Milestones may include specific training units, advertising a vacancy or sourcing an excellent company to outsource to.

Budget—You will need a budget to close the gap unless you undertake free training or self-education from websites like YouTube or specific technical websites. Determine the budget required for each gap and any resources needed to complete the tasks effectively.

Implement—It's time to implement your plans. By getting this far, you have thought strategically and developed a solid plan, secure in the knowledge that you have considered the priorities. Your plan has motivating milestones you can tick off as you achieve them.

Training—If you use training for any gaps, you will roll out training sessions, attend workshops, take online courses, or do in-person training. You can choose any learning that suits you, and blended learning techniques can cater to different learning styles and topics.

Recruitment—If recruiting someone to fill your skills gap is the best option, you should complete a strong job description with all the required skills and experience. Advertise the job opening, screen candidates, conduct interviews, and select the best candidate.

Outsourcing - Outsourcing is a good option, as it allows you to choose between self-training and hiring someone into your business. Here, you should research potential freelancers or companies that can assist you. Negotiate contracts that specify the details of the work, including timelines, what needs to be achieved and to what standard.

Monitor—Track the progress made, tick off your milestones, and adjust the content or format of your plans where needed. Not everything is right the first time.

Following the steps in this chapter, we have identified crucial gaps and prioritised them based on their impact on our business's success. We have identified where our skills need enhancement and laid out tailored strategies to bridge these gaps. Each strategy was chosen with careful consideration of our resources and long-term business objectives, ensuring that our efforts are both efficient and impactful.

As these strategies are implemented, the journey has started but is not yet complete. The actual test of our plans' effectiveness lies in their execution and measurable outcomes. Monitoring our success and adjusting our approaches based on our business needs will help our commitment to continuous improvement. As you move forward, remain proactive, responsive, and flexible.

4 Creating Compelling Job Descriptions

The desire to handle every aspect of your business is natural; you have a passion, unique skill set, and work ethic that are both strengths and potential bottlenecks. Trying to do everything yourself can hinder scaling and growth. Recognising when and how to delegate tasks effectively becomes crucial as your business grows.

In the previous section, we could see where our gaps lie and put them into groups, e.g. marketing or operations. You may undertake training for some tasks to close the gap; for others, you may outsource. For example, if you have a similar area of tasks, such as marketing, you may outsource this. For other areas, you may recruit an employee part-time, full-time or temporary.

In this section, we will examine creating job descriptions that capture the essence of each role. Entrepreneurs often possess a broad range of skills, but successful scaling involves recognising that you don't need to do everything yourself. Instead, it's about leveraging potential employees' specific strengths and specialisms.

Effective job descriptions enable you to delegate responsibilities wisely, ensuring that every task is managed by someone who is not just capable but also ideally suited to that role. By establishing realistic job descriptions tailored to your business's needs, you not only optimise operational efficiency but also create a foundation for sustainable growth.

Creating compelling job descriptions is a critical step in recruitment, ensuring you attract suitable candidates for your business needs. Here's a detailed guide to crafting clear and effective job descriptions.

Step 1: Understand the Role and Its Impact

Looking at your previous analysis of skills gaps in your business, you should have a picture of what tasks must be focused on. You could focus on the function with the most tasks, which may require a specialist. You may focus on those that will have the most impact on your business, either financially or time. This could be a salesperson or an administrative person taking over work that will free up your time. Use the information you uncovered to understand the specific needs of the role and how it will fit into your business as it grows.

Choose a broad job function - As this is a new role, you must decide where it fits. Is it a specialist role in a particular area, an operations role responsible for distributing your products or services, or an administrative role that will handle all the foundational work?

Document everything - You will likely already be completing some tasks in your day-to-day business. Document everything you do in this job role; you want a comprehensive list of all activities, required skills, and the impact on the company. This list will help form a job description and a list of tasks. Ideally, you should also create an operations manual for these tasks. An operations manual is a step-by-step guide that someone can pick up to know precisely what they need to do to complete the jobs you do. Completing this detailed task analysis will help you understand not only the position's day-to-day activities and the skills that will be necessary but also why these tasks are required to help the business achieve its goals. Consider if any soft skills are also required to complete this role. Soft skills can include communication or customer service. Software like Google Docs can be helpful to document everything as it is easily accessible and easily edited.

Alignment - Ensure that the role aligns with your overall business goals. Each task that the role contains should be able to be mapped back to the broader business objectives; this will help to make the role's impact clear and justified. You can share this with any new starters so that they can understand the role they play in the business objectives.

Identify key requirements - Assess what level of experience and educational background is required for the role. If it is an entry-level role, it will likely find hands-on experience is more important than a degree. Decide if you are willing to train some skills or if they need to come with the knowledge. If the task requires knowledge of an identified skills gap, you will want someone to arrive with it as a strength. Also, consider if the role requires soft skills, such as excellent communication or customer service. How well you can communicate these requirements in the job description will directly influence the quality of the applicants.

Review and refine - Once you have your requirements, structure the information into two parts. You want a list of the roles, responsibilities (the tasks), and requirements (any previous experience/qualifications).

Step 2: Define the Job Position Clearly

Moving on from the brief responsibilities and requirements, defining and creating the job clearly and precisely is essential. This step ensures that your potential candidates understand what the role entails and what they require to succeed. As your company grows, you will also include where it fits within the larger organisation.

We'll also discuss the importance of using language that resonates with the ideal candidate and promotes diversity and inclusiveness. This approach enhances the clarity of the job posting and strengthens our employer brand, attracting candidates with the right skills who will thrive within our team.

Use a job description template to give you a starting point to ensure all necessary information is included.

Reporting - Clearly define the job title and who the role reports to. You will want to ensure that the title of the role is realistic for the tasks that must be performed and its position within the organisation. Do not give a Head of Department name for a position that completes foundational admin activities. There is nothing to say that someone who takes an administrative role will not progress to the position of Head of Department, but it needs to be realistic concerning tasks, responsibilities, and pay. Some companies have fun job titles; however, this will not mean much to people outside your company looking for jobs. If this is the first supporting role in your business, they will likely report directly to you. If they report to someone else, detail what position they will report to, e.g. Administration Manager.

Roles and Responsibilities - Break down each central area of responsibility that you have identified and describe the tasks. When doing so, use action-oriented language to convey the duties, such as Manage, Create, Develop or Lead. These will help someone understand if they will be expected to follow the current set processes, whether they will be required to create something new or perhaps be responsible for looking after a particular set of work. Use bullet points to start each of these action-oriented responsibilities. Include how these tasks fit into the business's overall success where possible. An example could be to Manage incoming customer communications using the company email system to ensure a positive customer experience and potential repeat business. We want to avoid ambiguity and set clear expectations, so use tools like Grammarly to assist you with clarity and conciseness.

Specify required qualifications - List any necessary qualifications, including work experience, technical skills, and soft skills. Emphasis on necessary: do not request a qualification if it is not needed as a part of the job; you may alienate potential candidates. Be specific about the type and level of educational requirements, e.g. Do they require a Bachelor's degree in a related field, an apprenticeship or two years of working experience?

Highlight desired competencies - This is where you want to list the required and desired soft skills identified earlier. Put your essential requirements first, followed by the desired skills; this will help highlight skills that are a must-have versus those that are a nice-to-have. The skills you identified could be communication, leadership or problem-solving.

Inclusive language - Throughout this process, use inclusive language; you do not want to unconsciously deter many candidates from applying for the role. For example, using words like 'rockstar' or 'ninja' can make it look like you are trying to attract younger applicants.

Step 3: Highlight Company Culture and Benefits

As an entrepreneur starting to scale your business, you may not have considered what company culture is to you. You may well have a great idea of what you don't want it to be based on previous work experience. It does not need to be set in stone at this stage, but it would be a good idea to consider some 'values' that mean something to you; they can start forming your cultural values. This area is less about what you are looking for from your candidates but what you can offer to the top talent.

Company culture - Many job seekers seek more than just a role; they seek a work environment where they can thrive and whose values match the business's values. You can assess how well your candidates are aligned by thinking of what values mean something to you, with you and your business. Describe your company culture and how it supports growth, allowing you to sell your business as an attractive offer and position and attract top talent. Articulate what makes your company unique, whether it is your approach to something or the support you offer. Think about what it is that made you set up and go solo.

Benefits and perks - As a smaller company, you may not be in a position to offer as much as a multi-national organisation would be able to, and that is okay. While you may not be able to provide many tangible perks that cost additional money above a salary, you can provide intangible perks such as flexible working hours, remote working opportunities, and development opportunities. Different benefits and perks appeal to different people, so you may wish to keep your options open here.

5 Mastering the Interview Process

The interview is one of the most crucial elements in the recruitment process. At this point, you can assess whether your candidates will transform into your employees. Mastering this process is essential for identifying the most suitable candidates based on skills and experience and understanding how they might fit within and contribute to your organisation's culture and goals.

In this section, you will be guided through each phase of the interview process, from preparation to final decision-making. You will learn how to structure comprehensive and balanced interviews, exploring not only the candidates' competencies but also their alignment with your organisational values.

Whether you're conducting your first interview or looking to refine your techniques, the insights provided here will empower you to conduct more effective and meaningful interviews. We will discuss essential skills such as active listening and unbiased evaluation. By the end of this section, you will possess a comprehensive toolkit that will improve your hiring outcomes and enhance the candidate experience, reflecting positively on your company.

Effective preparation is crucial for a smooth interview execution and for setting the stage for a meaningful and insightful interview. This initial step, preparing for the interview, will lay the groundwork for successfully evaluating your candidates.

We will explore a mindset of curiosity and non-judgement, encouraging a deeper understanding of candidates beyond their curriculum vitae. The goal is to transform each interview into a two-way conversation that offers valuable insights into your candidates' abilities and what they can add to your organisation's culture.

Step 1: Prepare for the Interview

Review the application - Before the interview, ensure that you review your candidate's CV and application thoroughly so that you refresh your memory of who you are talking to and their experience. If they have included their online social profiles, like LinkedIn, you may wish to review these also to get a sense of their professional persona. Don't make assumptions about what you see on the CV, such as why they moved positions. You can use the interview to collect facts about the candidate and their experiences.

Question preparation - A good practice is to ask every candidate the same set of questions because you can say you have been consistent with every candidate. You can still ask logical follow-up questions as they arise, but your core questions should be the same to give everyone the same interview experience. While you will have a list of questions, the interview should be conversational, following the questions as a guide. At the start, I often let a candidate know that I have a set of questions I will be working through but that it will be more of a conversation. We want to take every interview as an opportunity to learn something new about someone's experiences and perspectives. Compile a list of questions to help you uncover how well your candidate matches the tasks in the job description and your other requirements. You may ask how they approach different scenarios to understand the logic they take, their experience, and how they solve problems. You might ask them to explain when they experienced a difficult customer situation and what approach they took to remedy it. By including open-ended questions, you should encourage your candidate to discuss their professional experience, motivation, and long-term career aspirations.

Set up the interview environment - A great interview should provide a comfortable, welcoming, and professional environment for candidates to express themselves, whether online or in person. You will want to be fully present, actively listening and engaging with candidates' responses. This will allow you to assess not just what is said but how it is said. We want it to be a two-way conversation, with candidates having the opportunity to ask questions throughout. First interviews are ideally conducted online using a tool like Zoom or Microsoft Teams, allowing you to assess more candidates regardless of their location. Ensure you familiarise yourself with the software beforehand and sign in five to ten minutes before the interview so you are on time and do not leave the candidate waiting. Sometimes technology fails, so it is a good idea to have your candidate's telephone number so you can switch to a telephone call if needed. For face-to-face interviews, ensure your chosen room is quiet, comfortable and free from distractions.

Step 2: Conduct the Interview

Conducting the interview takes you from theory to practice, you can engage directly with candidates and assess their suitability for the role.

Starting the interview - It is advisable to start your interview by making your candidate comfortable. I thank them for attending and ask if they are ready to start. This gives you permission to start and the candidate the opportunity to decline should something come up. You want your candidates to be at their best; sometimes, that may mean rearranging the interview. Let them know that you plan to take notes throughout the interview.

Structured questioning - Start a conversational flow to be able to work through your questions. This is your opportunity to ask the technical and behavioural questions you devised in the last section to understand your candidate's abilities and try to stick to the same questions in the same order. You will still be able to have the ability to probe deeper into your candidate's responses while looking for verbal and non-verbal clues in their responses to assess how they handle different situations.

The STAR technique - The STAR technique is an approach to asking questions to get a detailed insight into candidates' past experiences and behaviours. You will use the same questions you created but format it as (Situation, Task, Action, Result). Use your question to present a 'Situation' and ask your candidate to explain a similar task, what 'Actions' they took and the end 'Result'. This will allow you to assess how the candidate approaches situations, their problem-solving abilities, and their self-awareness. Repeat this for each of your questions. Again, you can still explore their responses with follow-up questions.

Documenting - Ensure you take detailed notes during the interview; if you have a good typing speed, you can use something accessible like Google Docs. I note the candidates' main points, but I can type quickly. If you are not so quick, you could make key notes about how they approached the STAR method and whether they achieved the outcome. You need to be able to ensure that you can accurately compare candidates after the interview. You can also use this opportunity to make a brief note to rate each response. Whatever method you use, you need to be consistent across candidates. The key point may be them achieving the task, taking a particular approach, highlighting that they have the ability to cover a particular gap that you have, or it could be demonstrating one of the soft skills required for the role. Customise your own rating scale for each key question, competency or skill required for the role.

Step 3: Evaluate the Candidates

Once you have interviewed all the potential candidates through a structured interview process, you enter a pivotal stage of evaluating them. This is a critical step as it involves a thorough assessment of all the information gathered to ensure that our hiring decisions are not only informed but also fair and aligned with your business goals.

Review notes - List the candidate's strengths and weaknesses using your notes and the rating system you created. While skills are important, they can also be taught, so ensure that you prioritise someone's cultural fit, what they will add to the culture and their growth potential. Remember, we need to be consistent when evaluating our candidates to ensure that we are fair. Value diverse perspectives, backgrounds and experiences as they can enhance creativity and innovation within your business. Consider consulting with other trusted people, presenting all the information, and gaining their thoughts.

Final selection - Once a decision has been made based on the required criteria, select the candidate who best fits the culture and meets the role's requirements. Prepare to offer the position to the chosen candidate, ensuring you have all the necessary offer paperwork and background checks ready.

Step 4: Provide Feedback and Close the Loop

As you conclude the interview process, providing feedback and closing the loop with every candidate is good practice. This is where we demonstrate our commitment to transparency, ensuring that each candidate receives thoughtful feedback regardless of the outcome. It is a respectful opportunity to reinforce a positive perception of your company, even among those who do not join your business. Commit to treating every candidate with the utmost respect, recognising that today's applicant could be tomorrow's client, customer or team member.

Gather your feedback - Soon after you finish the interviews, schedule some time in your diary to draft personalised feedback for each candidate. You can use an overall template for your responses to speed up the process, but you should personalise elements to reflect on the specific interactions you had. It is sensible to have a series of emails to offer the position, provide constructive feedback if requested, and gently reject feedback. The emails should be warm in nature and communicate your appreciation for the candidates' time and effort.

Inform successful candidate - This is the exciting part where you can offer the position; for speed and clarity, I suggest the initial offer is a phone call. Give them a call, introduce yourself, say that you would like to offer them the position of [Job title], and tell them the pay rate you would like to offer. In an ideal world, they will enthusiastically accept, at which point you can let them know you will send the formal offer via email for them to respond to. If they want to take a few days to think about it, that is fair, but give them a deadline; otherwise, everyone will be waiting. Your initial offer letter/email will contain the formalities of the job offer, requesting them to reply to confirm that they accept. If they decline the offer on the phone, gently probe what would have made them accept the offer; you may be able to meet them halfway. Offering jobs is often a negotiation. Don't delay on this step, your candidate would likely be interviewing elsewhere at the same time and may also receive other offers.

Decline other candidates - When you have your acceptance from your chosen candidate, it is time to decline the other candidates. Ensure that you inform them of their status as soon as possible; delaying negative feedback can increase anxiety for some. Use a standard email template to decline people, with an offer to provide more specific feedback if they would like it. For those who performed really well, consider offering that feedback as a phone call. For candidates who were in the final stages of your interview process, who were a very close fit, consider offering to retain their details for a short period of time, eg 12 months, should other roles arise, then you can contact them and offer them the ability to apply. You should seek their permission to retain their details and contact them in the future.

Providing feedback - If a candidate requests feedback, focus on the strengths they demonstrated during the interview; if appropriate, you can provide specific areas for improvement. Feedback should be constructive and clear so that it will assist the candidate's professional growth. Understand that the interview process may have been a lot for your candidates. They may have been heavily invested in getting the role, and they may struggle to receive feedback, so only provide it if requested.

Continuous improvement - Creating a culture of continuous improvement will be beneficial to your business improvement. By requesting anonymous feedback at the end of the recruitment process, you will gain valuable insights into how the process was for your candidates, where you can make improvements if needed. You can use a tool like Google Forms to collect feedback without contact details. By regularly reflecting, you can ensure that your communication style is inclusive, respectful and encouraging.

6 Implementing Effective Onboarding and Integration

Congratulations, you have your first employee! An effective onboarding process is crucial to ensure your new hire transitions smoothly into their role and quickly becomes a productive member of the team. Onboarding is not just about filling in forms; it's about creating a welcoming environment that supports long-term engagement and success. This is more than a procedural exercise; it is an opportunity to enhance employee experience and engagement from day one.

This initial step in the onboarding process sets the foundation for your new employees' understanding of their role, the company culture, and the company's expectations of them. It can be tempting to put your new employee straight to work; you likely hired them because you have a need. However, take your time getting them started. Even if they seem keen, you want to ensure they are gently fed into the business and taught everything they need to know.

Step 1: Design the Onboarding Plan

Objective gathering - Previously, we uncovered the role's objectives and gathered these as the skills that your new hire will need to perform their job effectively. You will need to decide on some performance objectives, being specific about what your new hire should be able to achieve after the first week, month and quarter. They need to have clear and measurable outcomes. Also, consider if there are any cultural values that your new hire will need to demonstrate; these could be linked to your company's cultural values.

Develop content - Creating modules that are focused on different aspects of the business and the role will ensure that everything is covered; it should be informative and welcoming. Each module should have a specific learning outcome that you expect to be achieved. Create content covering any company policies you have, information on your company culture, how you came to create your business (your mission, vision and values), compliance and safety. If you have any key people within your business, you can take this opportunity to introduce them as a part of the induction process. You will also need to have content that is specific to the role. Your content should include engaging learning experiences for adults, using a mix of instructional techniques, scenarios, simulations mimicking real job tasks, hands-on projects, and collaborative learning. Having a hard copy your new starter can refer to is important. It also allows you to demonstrate the information to them and cater to different learning styles.

Structuring the timeline - Design the onboarding timeline in phases; ideally, the first day or even week does not include actual work; it is a better experience to learn about the company and get eased into the work process. Start with general orientation, move on to role-specific training and then move on to ongoing development. You typically have three months to expect someone to have achieved all your learning outcomes, getting closer to being up to full speed. Plan a timeline for the first week, month, and three months, including key milestones and goals for them to achieve during this time. Schedule regular check-ins to discuss progress, address concerns, and adjust the onboarding plan as needed. This is your core onboarding for this role; it is time to customise it based on your specific new starter.

Step 2: Personalise the Onboarding Experience

By taking the time to invest in personalising each aspect of the onboarding experience, we can align it with the unique backgrounds, skills, and expectations of your new hire. No two hires are the same. This will allow you to address their needs and enhance their engagement and connection with your company from day one, increasing employee retention and satisfaction.

Gather information - Before your employee starts and after signing their contract, send a detailed survey for your new hire to complete before their start date. This should include questions like what their preferred learning style is (visual, auditory, hands-on); they should be able to include any previous knowledge they have that is relevant to their new role and ask them what they hope to gain from the onboarding process and if they have any initial concerns or personal goals. You could offer to complete this as an informal conversation, either in person or virtually, if they would prefer. Ensure to reassure them that this process is to help build the best onboarding experience for them.

Adapt the onboarding plan - Once you have your questions answered by your new starter, use the data to identify if they have any specific needs and preferences. Customise the schedule to cater to their learning style and interests. Ensure that you schedule in time to review how the onboarding is going; at the end of each module, your new hire should have the opportunity to discuss if they feel they have achieved and understand the objectives, if they would like more support in this area and have the flexibility to add additional training or move the training around. By having a flexible onboarding experience, you can spend more time on topics they may find more challenging or interesting.

Step 3: Feedback

In previous sections, we sought feedback following the recruitment process; the same should be done for the onboarding process. You can devise anonymous feedback forms to collect information on improving the process. Now, if this is your first employee, it will not be anonymous, so ensure that you create a safe space for someone to provide feedback on the basis that it is being used to improve the process for next time. Good times to gather this feedback are after the first week, the first month, and three months.

7 Maintenance

Scaling your business is not a do once and done achievement; it requires ongoing growth, learning and adaptation to sustain the growth. You should pay attention to some core areas to assist you.

Fostering a Positive Company Culture

Now you are officially a leader of people, its even more important to act like one by ensuring that you promote clearly your vision, mission and values, these serve as the foundation to your company culture. In your leadership, you should encourage input from all levels, move away from having a top down approach to one that is inclusive. Trusting your team with the responsibilities that you have given them, letting them have the sense of ownership and being open to their feedback and ideas will help create a culture of continuous improvement. While you may have the big ideas, often, great insights come from those completing the actual work. So regularly seek and act on feedback from your team and celebrate achievements as they arise to reinforce positive behaviours.

Setting up Effective Communication Systems

Everyone has preferred communication methods, and you will not know them, nor will they know yours, unless you let each other know. Make it clear how often you would like communications on different aspects of the job and in what method. You can use platforms like Slack to keep track of conversations and use it as the starting point for celebrating success and navigating challenges as a team. The default should be transparency without repercussions, not penalising people when minor things go wrong. It is essential to build a culture of trust.

Systems like Clickup, Asana, or Trello can help manage tasks and projects. When set up correctly, they can notify different people of the progress of tasks and when the next person is expected to start their part of a task.

Implement regular check-ins and meetings with proactive communication to share updates, celebrate successes and discuss challenges.

Continuously Evaluating and Addressing Skills Gaps

In the first part of this guide, you successfully found the current skills gaps in your business, but guess what? Skills gaps evolve and should be addressed on an ongoing basis. Forward planning is ideal here. Consider and anticipate future trends in your industry, assess your business's evolving needs, and identify new skill requirements. As your business grows, you will find that the business needs change. By following this feedback loop to the start of this guide regularly, you can plan for upskilling and reskilling regularly. Continuous improvement and skill development is valued and supported.

8 FAQs

What if I conduct a skills gap analysis and discover too many?

Finding out that you have more skills gaps than you anticipated can be overwhelming, but it does not have to be a problem with further strategic thinking.

You can prioritise based on how critical and urgent they are. If you have a gap vital to your business operating immediately, then they will be the ones you focus on upskilling for immediately. If you have an urgent gap due to a current project, then you can shift your attention to that one. Then you can further segment the skills based on whether they are for short term success or long term growth, you may find that going for the short term success in the interim will help move your business forward to then being able to focus on long term growth.

How often should I conduct a skills gap analysis?

It is advisable to undertake some form of business planning every year. In this process, you should conduct a comprehensive skills gap analysis per your business plans and financial budget.
You should then quarterly review and update your analysis to address immediate changes or emerging needs.
If your business experiences significant changes, such as technological changes, changes in the market, or changes in people's roles, then this is another time to review your analysis.

Monitor your analysis regularly, at least once a month, when you have your employee catch-up sessions to assess progress in closing the gaps.

What if I can't afford to hire right now?

Step one in considering hiring people should constantly be assessing where you can automate repetitive tasks using software to assist you in freeing up your time for more strategic thinking.

If you have done this and have gone through your finances and can see that you are not yet in a position to hire someone full-time or part-time, consider outsourcing some work on a project basis. Outsourcing to a freelancer or contract worker will mean giving someone a set amount of work to complete within a set price and timeline.

You may find that you can barter your services with other people in your network, swapping skills with each other to get work completed.

Consider hiring an apprentice/intern to help you. This position usually takes place while the person is gaining an education. It is worth noting that if you go this route, you will not be able to hand over work and leave them to it. You must invest time into them to help them get up to speed.

How do I create job descriptions for roles I'm not familiar with?

When you explore which tasks are required, your job description will start to form itself. You may find that if you were to look up a similar job description, your position does not have all the same requirements, and that is OK. You only need to list what you need to be completed at this present time; roles can evolve and grow.

Use a template to help guide you through what should be included and benchmark the position against similar positions in your region to assist you.

How can I tell if a candidate is a good cultural fit during interviews?

Be clear on your culture. At interviews, you can ask candidates behavioural questions to understand how people approach different situations. This will help you see if they follow similar values to yours. The same can be said for hypothetical situational questions, probing how they would deal with the scenario. You can also ask about their personal values to understand what means a lot to them and look for consistency throughout.

If a candidate excels technically but seems to lack soft skills, should I still consider them?

There is a saying that you can teach technical skills, so hire for soft skills; while this could be approach number one, don't dismiss someone immediately if they seem to lack soft skills. You may find they have the skills but struggle to demonstrate them in an interview setting. Then assess whether the role requires them to have those skills, if they will not be customer facing, they will likely not need to be incredibly outgoing to be good at their job. Discuss also if they are willing to work on those soft skills if you are willing to put in the time to support them.

How do I ensure the interview process is unbiased?

In the previous section, we discussed ensuring that all interviews follow the same format. Having a standardised process with the same set of questions is a solid starting point. If you are able to bring in a diverse group of people to assist you with reviewing applications, that would be good, even more so if you are able to remove any identifying details from the application.

What if I hire the wrong person?

Hiring mistakes happen for different reasons but are unlikely to occur repeatedly if you note what went wrong and what could have been done differently. When you face issues, there are some sensible steps you can take.

Early intervention: The sooner you address the problem, the better. That doesn't have to mean getting rid of them and giving up straight away. Sit down with the employee and talk to them about the specific unaligned areas of their performance or behaviours within the role or your company. This can be completed as part of the probationary period process.

Assess and adjust responsibilities: Sometimes, it's not the person who is the problem but the role, especially when it is new to the company, or there have been recent changes. Take a look at the role and see where it can be improved. Does it fit within one person's abilities, or could it work better if it were split into two? Assess whether aspects of the job can be adjusted to better match the employee's strengths.

Implement a Performance Improvement Plan (PIP): This structured plan sets clear expectations and supports improvement. If you create one, ensure that it includes specific, measurable goals and a timeline for reassessment.

Provide support and training: Your onboarding should consider not only what your employee needs to know about the company but also a granular level of how you do the tasks within your business. This should allow your employees to work to your standards but do not use it to stifle innovation. Identify what areas your employees might benefit from additional training or mentoring. By investing in development, you can turn situations around. Regularly review processes together to see if there are better ways to do things.

Make a tough decision if necessary: If, after giving time and support, you decide that the fit is not right, you may find it is time to part ways. You need to ensure that you handle this process respectfully and legally. If you have been transparent with the improvements needed up to this point, it should not surprise the employee if it does not work out.

How can I trust someone else with my vision?

Trust can be challenging to give to people you do not know, I get it, but it is important that you do so that you can start freeing yourself up to cover other areas of your business.

Articulating your vision to others in a clear, compelling way will help ensure that your new starter understands what your business does, how it achieves success and the why behind your business. By bringing them along in your journey and embedding your culture into everything you do, you will be closer to them fully understanding your vision. Earlier, it was mentioned that it should be clear why every task in the business is completed and how it helps get closer to the overall goal (vision); taking the time to explain helps with growing a team invested in the business.

You should also lead by example. There is little point in having values that you do not demonstrate yourself; that is the quickest way to someone losing passion within your company. When your team sees you living the vision and values, they are more likely to do the same.

Empower your team to make decisions within their areas of responsibility. This will help them take some ownership and invest personally in the vision. While sometimes things will not always go to plan, creating an open environment where mistakes are seen as opportunities to learn and shared will encourage innovation and initiative.

Continue to check in with your team and have frequent discussions about how they are doing and how the work they are completing contributes to the company goals. This will help keep the vision front of mind and allow for corrections as needed.

How do I handle onboarding remotely?

For the most part, follow the same onboarding process as we highlighted earlier; you will need to ensure that they have any equipment before their first day and be able to set themselves up. Set clear expectations for day one; they may complete less work and spend more time finding out where things are online. You may choose to have them start later to accept equipment delivery and set themselves up with any passwords. Plan in more contact points each day initially, they will not have the opportunity to ask adhoc questions unless you have a virtual training session.

What if a new hire doesn't meet the expectations after onboarding?

Having regular contact points throughout the onboarding period should prevent this from happening. By ensuring that you address issues directly as they happen and providing specific examples of underperformance, they will be able to work towards clearly defined expectations. It may be that external factors are causing problems. Seek to understand if this is the case so that you can help them work around the problems.

If, despite the above, you still face problems, consider extending the probationary period for one to three months further. Be sure you are clear on what is not being achieved and what you expect to achieve to pass the probation and secure employment.

How can I make my job descriptions stand out to top talent?

Keep your job description clear and concise, and use bullet points to make it visually easier to read. If possible, have a compelling introduction with a strong attention-grabbing headline. Ensure you highlight the benefits, culture, values, and growth opportunities available for working in your business. Be authentic in your job description to attract similar people. If you portray your company in a way that it is not, people will not be aligned.

How can I avoid procrastinating with this process?

When you have a million things to do in your business, it is easy to procrastinate and avoid tasks, even when they will help you in the long run.

Break your tasks into smaller chunks of work that are more manageable and less overwhelming. Set yourself clear deadlines and accountability. If that works for you, consider getting an accountability partner who can keep you on track.

Tools like the Pomodoro technique can help. In this technique, you work in 25-minute bursts and take 5 minutes in between for rest. This can help increase productivity and reduce burnout.

You could create a stop-doing list until you manage to reach certain milestones of this project. That list would include items that are taking up too much time or are no longer necessary.

I'm not sure I can do this, what should I do?

Firstly, you can! Reframe any negative self-talk, try to spot any negative patterns, and challenge the thoughts. There may be underlying fears or doubts within you. Identify them and work through those doubts by developing strategies to overcome them. Believe in your abilities. You have come this far through your intelligence, hard work, dedication, and persistence. You will be able to continue with your curiosity and resilience.

9 Outro

As you conclude "Hidden Skills: Uncovering What Your Business Really Needs," you've moved towards understanding and transforming your entrepreneurial adventures. We have equipped you with essential insights and strategies to propel your business to new heights.

By conducting a skill gap analysis, you now understand the critical skills your business needs and can pinpoint areas for growth. This foundational step allows you to plan and develop the capabilities required for sustainable success strategically.

We've debunked common myths surrounding entrepreneurship throughout. Overnight success is a rare exception, not the rule. True success is built on hard work, dedication, and strategic planning.

You've learned how to create compelling job descriptions that attract the right talent, master the interview process to ensure technical competence and cultural alignment and implement effective onboarding procedures that help new hires integrate and become productive quickly. These hiring strategies are designed to build a strong, cohesive team that drives your business forward.

Continuous improvement is the cornerstone of lasting success. Regularly evaluating and addressing skill gaps, fostering a positive company culture, and staying adaptable to market changes are vital for maintaining a competitive edge. Committing to ongoing learning and development ensures your business remains resilient and poised for growth.

Now, it's time to take action. Implement the strategies you've learned and watch as your business transforms into a more efficient, scalable, and resilient enterprise. Trust in the process and believe in your ability to achieve remarkable success. Every step you take now brings you closer to realizing your entrepreneurial dreams and enjoying the work-life balance you deserve.

You've taken the crucial first step by absorbing the insights in this book. The future of your business is in your hands. Take action now, and pave the way for a thriving, prosperous future. Embrace the journey ahead with confidence and hope, knowing that your business will flourish beyond your expectations with dedication and the right strategies. Start today, and let your business reach new heights of growth and success.

ABOUT THE AUTHOR

Roxanne Massey is a CIPD-qualified Human Resources professional with over 20 years of experience.

Unconsciously, she started her career in HR and recruitment, perhaps inspired by her father's former HR career or her aunt's recruitment business. Not realising that a passion for helping others and doing the right thing for people was bubbling inside.

Studying for her degree in Business created an additional spark, which has seen her helping micro-companies and industry-leading mega-corporations across many sectors. She motivates, guides and ensures the right people are in the right place at the right time.

When Roxanne isn't improving working environments, she can be found with her four children in her London home, trying to raise them into people ready to take on the world.

www.ingramcontent.com/pod-product-compliance
Lightning Source LLC
Chambersburg PA
CBHW050018230526
45470CB00003B/1023